Someone I Like

Poems About People

For Alistair James Blance, with love — J.N.
A Miriam e alla sua mamma — G.M.

Barefoot Books Ltd
124 Walcot Street
Bath
BA1 5BG

This book was typeset in Optima and FrizQuadrata
The illustrations were prepared in china ink and watercolour
on 100% cotton 300gsm watercolour paper

Graphic design by Tom Grzelinski, Bath
Colour separation by Grafiscan, Verona
Printed and bound in Singapore by Tien Wah Press (Pte) Ltd

This book has been printed on 100% acid-free paper

Paperback ISBN 1 84148 005 3

British Cataloguing-in-Publication Data: a catalogue record
for this book is available from the British Library

1 3 5 7 9 8 6 4 2

Someone I Like

Poems About People

compiled by Judith Nicholls

illustrated by Giovanni Manna

Barefoot Books
Celebrating Art and Story

Contents

INTRODUCTION

I have shared poetry with children of all ages and in hundreds of schools. Of all the letters I have received after these visits, one particular note has remained on my study wall, irresistibly, for some years now. It's in the large, painstaking print of a beginner-writer called John and says simply: *Thos powims wur gud!*

This is a typical response; *all* young children love wordplay. They love to *hear* it from the time they are babes-in-arms, they love to *read* it as soon as they can, they love to *try* it for themselves. The youngest children love especially those first-recognisable attributes of poetry: rhyme and rhythm — hence the enduring popularity of nursery and traditional rhymes with their close affinity to music. *Rhyme, rhythm, repetition, alliteration*: these are just a few of the ingredients that help to make poems memorable. The child who becomes familiar with some of these patterns also has a head-start as an independent reader.

The theme of this anthology is relationships — a subject none of us can escape, and something we all begin to learn about from the moment we are born. In 'My Little Sister', Moira Andrew expresses an ambivalence about the arrival of a new sibling in a way all of us can identify with, while Elizabeth Jennings explores the mystery of having an imaginary playmate in 'The Secret Brother'. The simplicity of Vyanne Samuels's 'Daddy' manages to express in just four lines the developing realisation that perhaps a parent is not *quite* perfect after all...

Compare Gwendolyn Brooks's 'André' and Hiawyn Oram's 'Urgent Note to My Parents', which add a further dimension to the same topic.

Humour is a vital ingredient of happy relationships, and a good starting point for children who are exploring poetry. Mary Ann Hoberman's 'Brother' has a tongue-twisting quality which is full of wordplay and cries out for a good performance, as does David Whitehead's 'Kissing Auntie' and John Agard's 'High Heels'.

A good poem can also help us to approach the unapproachable. Kit Wright's 'Grandad' is a wonderful example of how the simplest, everyday words can be chosen and ordered in a way that is charged with feelings and far more moving than something flowery or complex could ever be.

A wonderful example of poetry speaking across barriers of time and of place is 'Oath of Friendship'. Only recently I read this poem to a group of teachers and librarians and asked them to guess when it was written; no-one did. This poem, in spite of its immediacy, hails from China in the first century B.C.!

I hope that you will enjoy sharing these poems with the children close to you and that they, too, will conclude *Thos powims wur gud!*

Judith Nicholls

Oath of Friendship

SHANG YA!
I want to be your friend
For ever and ever without break or decay.
When the hills are all flat
And the rivers are all dry,
When it lightens and thunders in winter,
When it rains and snows in summer,
When Heaven and Earth mingle —
Not till then will I part from you.

Anon., translated by Arthur Waley

two friends

lydia and shirley have
two pierced ears and
two bare ones
five pigtails
two pairs of sneakers
two berets
two smiles
one necklace
one bracelet
lots of stripes and
one good friendship

Nikki Giovanni

My Hard Repair Job

In the awful quarrel
we had, my temper burnt
our friendship to cinders.
How can I make it whole again?

This way, that way,
that time, this time,
I pick up the burnt bits,
trying to change them back.

James Berry

11

Someone I Like

Someone I like is far away,
I feel the silence everywhere.
I didn't know how much I'd care.
Someone I like is far away,
I feel the silence in the air,
I feel it, feel it

        everywhere.

Charlotte Zolotow

André

I had a dream last night. I dreamed
I had to pick a Mother out
I had to choose a Father too.
At first, I wondered what to do,
There were so many there, it seemed,
Short and tall and thin and stout.

But just before I sprang awake,
I knew what parents I would take.

And *this* surprised and made me glad:
They were the ones I always had!

Gwendolyn Brooks

Hugs and Kisses

Hugs and hugs and kisses...
Doesn't she know that I'm a boy?
Hugs and hugs and kisses...
I'm not some cuddly toy.
Hugs and hugs and kisses...
Boys should be treated rough.
Hugs and hugs and kisses...
These muscles show I'm tough.

Hugs and hugs and kisses...
Makes me want to run and hide.
I can't show the world how warm
Her hugs and hugs and kisses
Makes me feel...inside.

Lindamichellebaron

14

Urgent Note to My Parents

Don't ask me to do what I can't do
Only ask me to do what I can
Don't ask me to be what I can't be
Only ask me to be what I am

Don't one minute say 'Be a big girl'
and the next 'You're too little for that'
PLEASE don't ask me to be where I can't be
PLEASE be happy with right where I'm at

Hiawyn Oram

First Thing Today

(for Jimmy)

First thing today before
the cockerel crowed —
a baby's cry from
across the road.

Hi there baby,
damp and furled,
hi there. Welcome
to our world.

Here's the little finger
of my right hand
and here's a teddy
you won't understand

    yet

        and

          here's

flowers for your mummy
and what about this?
Here's my first hug
and my first kiss.

Fred Sedgwick

My Little Sister

They said they'd let me
hold her in the garden
for a photograph.

'Be careful,' they said.
'She's new and tiny
and very very precious.'

They sat me on a chair,
my legs dangling.
'Ready now?' they asked.

And they placed her
on my lap, wriggling and wet.
'Smile,' they said.

I tried, but it wasn't easy
to hold the baby and smile,
both at the same time.

Moira Andrew

Brother

I had a little brother
And I brought him to my mother
And I said I want another
Little brother for a change.
But she said don't be a bother
So I took him to my father
And I said this little bother
Of a brother's very strange.

But he said one little brother
Is exactly like another
And every little brother
Misbehaves a bit he said.
So I took the little bother
From my mother and my father
And I put the little bother
Of a brother back to bed.

Mary Ann Hoberman

High Heels

I wonder
how it feels
to wear high heels
like my big sister?

'Coz I'm smaller
I have to wait
longer
for high heels
to make me taller.

I wonder
how it feels
to wear high heels
and have corns
on your toes
and a blister?

I suppose
I'd better
ask my big sister.

John Agard

Daddy

Me so small
And you so tall,
Why can't you get the stars
From the sky after all?

Vyanne Samuels

Changing Places

It's strange to think
that my Grandad
is *Dad* to Dad.

When *I'm* a Dad,
will Dad be glad
to be *Grandad*?

Judith Nicholls

What Rachel Said

My grandchild looked at my grey, grey hair.
Her eyes were round in her head.
You'll have to be dying soon, Granny,
Won't you, Granny? she said.

I'd like to be staying a wee bit longer
— If you don't mind, said I.
I've poems to write, and flowers to grow,
And it's early yet to die.

But babies have to be born, Granny!
And you've had your turn, you see.
You'll have to make room for somebody new.
But I'll miss you, Granny, said she.

Lydia Pender

Granny

It so nice to have a Granny
when you've had it from yuh Mammy
and you feeling down and dammy

It so nice to have a Granny
when she brings you bread and jammy
and says, 'Tell it all to Granny.'

Grace Nichols

Grandad

Grandad's dead
And I'm sorry about that.

He'd a huge black overcoat.
He felt proud in it.
You could have hidden
A football crowd in it.
Far too big —
It was a lousy fit
But Grandad didn't
Mind a bit.
He wore it all winter
With a squashed black hat.

Now he's dead
And I'm sorry about that.

He'd got twelve stories.
I'd heard every one of them
Hundreds of times
But that was the fun of them:
You knew what was coming
So you could join in.
He'd got big hands
And brown, grooved skin
And when he laughed
It knocked you flat.

Now he's dead
And I'm sorry about that.

                    Kit Wright

End of a Holiday

My father climbs the stairs
Above my head
And then I hear him climb
Into his bed.

Sheep bleat — the sun's last sparks
Float through the wood
Like bubbles in last week's
Old lemonade.

I wait, and then I ask
Is he all right
Up in the dark without
A proper light.

He pulls the heavy clothes
Up to his chin.
I'm fine, he says, I'm perfect.
— Goodnight, son.

Ian Hamilton Finlay

Lineage

My grandmothers were strong.
They followed ploughs and bent to toil.
They moved through fields sowing seed.
They touched earth and grain grew.
They were full of sturdiness and singing.

My grandmothers are full of memories
Smelling of soap and onions and wet clay
With veins rolling roughly over quick hands
They have many clean words to say.
My grandmothers were strong.
Why am I not as they?

Margaret Walker

Reasons Why

Just because I loves you —
That's de reason why
Ma soul is full of colour
Like de wings of a butterfly.

Just because I loves you
That's de reason why
Ma heart's a fluttering aspen leaf
When you pass by.

Langston Hughes

To a New Brother

How many weeks have we been brothers?
You can't say. But one day,
When I've taught you to count,
You'll amaze them all.
That's what big brothers are for.

What's your name?
You don't even know that. Not yet.
But when we've practised it enough together
You will, I'm sure.
That's what big brothers are for.

And when you're older you'll be able
To join in so many of my games.
And sometimes, kid brother,
I'll let you choose
What we should play.

For I remember how it feels
To be the smallest like you.
And I know you'll find this
Difficult to believe,
But I was young once too.

Frances Nagle

The Secret Brother

Jack lived in the green-house
When I was six,
With glass and with tomato plants,
Not with slates and bricks.

I didn't have a brother,
Jack became mine.
Nobody could see him,
He never gave a sign.

Just beyond the rockery,
By the apple-tree,
Jack and his old mother lived,
Only for me.

With a tin telephone
Held beneath the sheet,
I would talk to Jack each night.
We would never meet.

Once my sister caught me,
Said, 'He isn't there.
Down among the flower-pots
Cramm the gardener

Is the only person.'
I said nothing, but
Let her go on talking.
Yet I moved Jack out.

He and his mother
Did a midnight flit.
No one knew his number:
I had altered it.

Only I could see
The sagging washing-line
And my brother making
Our own secret sign.

Elizabeth Jennings

Love Don't Mean

Love don't mean all that kissing
Like on television
Love means Daddy
Saying keep your mama company
    till I get back
And me doing it

Eloise Greenfield

People

Some people talk and talk
and never say a thing.
Some people look at you
and birds begin to sing.

Some people laugh and laugh
and yet you want to cry.
Some people touch your hand
and music fills the sky.

Charlotte Zolotow

Kissing Auntie

When Auntie tries to kiss me
I always hope she'll miss me.

Although she's nice
And smells of spice,
And eau de cologne
And talcum

I'd rather kiss cousin Malcolm!

David Whitehead

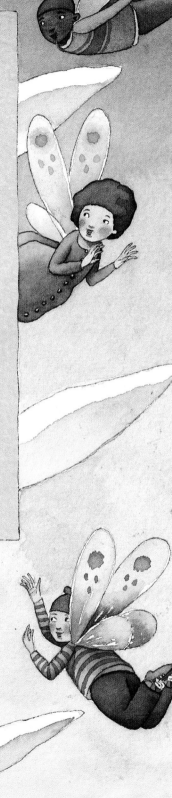

Story Time

When our teacher tells us stories
at the end of every day,
we all sit in silence
as she takes us far away.

To places where wise wizards
live in castles in the sky,
to lands where all the children
have wings so they can fly.

We all sit in silence
we just sit and stare,
for when teacher tells us stories
she makes us feel we're there.

Andrew Collett

Best Friend

When there's just one square
of chocolate left...
she shares,
she gives me half.

When thunder growls like an angry bear
and I shiver and shake
beneath my chair...
she won't laugh.

When I'm grumpy or cross
or spotty or sad,
when I whine or boss...
she stays.

When things aren't fair
and I hurt inside,
when I just want to hide...
she's there,
always.

Judith Nicholls

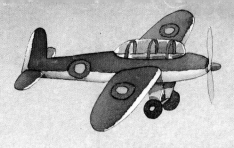

ACKNOWLEDGEMENTS

'Oath of Friendship', from *Chinese Poems* (George Allen & Unwin, 1946), translated by Arthur Waley, reproduced by kind permission of the Arthur Waley Estate; 'two friends' from *Spin a Soft Black Song* by Nikki Giovanni, copyright © 1985 by Nikki Giovanni. Reprinted by permission of Hill and Wang, a division of Farrar, Straus and Giroux, LLC; 'My Hard Repair Job' from *When I Dance* by James Berry. Reprinted by permission of The Peters Fraser and Dunlop Group Limited on behalf of James Berry, copyright © 1988; 'Someone I Like' from *Everything Glistens and Everything Sings* by Charlotte Zolotow, copyright © 1987 by Charlotte Zolotow. Reprinted by permission of S©ott Treimel New York; 'André' by Gwendolyn Brooks; 'Hugs and Kisses' by Lindamichellebaron; 'Urgent Note to My Parents' by Hiawyn Oram, copyright © Hiawyn Oram 1992, reproduced by kind permission of the author; 'First Thing Today' by Fred Sedgwick, copyright © Fred Sedgwick, reproduced by kind permission of the author; 'My Little Sister' by Moira Andrew, copyright © Moira Andrew, first published in *At Home and Next Door*, Riverpoint Publishing, 1998, reproduced by kind permission of the author; 'Brother' by Mary Ann Hoberman; 'High Heels' from *I Din Do Nuttin*, copyright © John Agard. Published by Bodley Head; 'Daddy' from *Beam*, copyright © 1990 Vyanne Samuels. Published by Methuen Children's Books and Mammoth, imprints of Egmont Children's Books Limited, London and used with permission; 'Changing Places' by Judith Nicholls, copyright © Judith Nicholls 2000, reprinted by kind permission of the author; 'What Rachel Said' by Lydia Pender; 'Granny' by Grace Nichols. Reproduced with permission of Curtis Brown Ltd, London, on behalf of Grace Nichols. Copyright © Grace Nichols 1991; 'Grandad' from *Rabbiting On* by Kit Wright, Fontana Lions 1978. Copyright © Kit Wright. Reproduced by kind permission of the author; 'End of a Holiday' by Ian Hamilton Finlay; 'Lineage' by Margaret Walker; 'Reasons Why' from *The Dream Keeper and Other Poems* by Langston Hughes copyright © Langston Hughes, published by Vintage; 'To a New Brother' from *You can't call a hedgehog Hopscotch* by Frances Nagle, copyright © Frances Nagle, published by Dagger Press, reproduced by kind permission of the author; 'The Secret Brother' from *Collected Poems* by Elizabeth Jennings, copyright © Elizabeth Jennings, published by Carcanet; 'Love Don't Mean' by Eloise Greenfield; 'People' from *River Winding* by Charlotte Zolotow, copyright © 1970 by Charlotte Zolotow. Reprinted by permission of S©ott Treimel New York; 'Kissing Auntie' by David Whitehead, copyright © David Whitehead, reproduced by kind permission of the author; 'Story Time' by Andrew Collett, copyright © Andrew Collett, reproduced by kind permission of the author; 'Best Friend' by Judith Nicholls, copyright © Judith Nicholls 2000, reprinted by kind permission of the author.

The publishers have made every effort to contact holders of copyright material. If you have not received our correspondence, please contact us for inclusion in future editions.